Rainy Day Appliqué

Quick & Easy Fusible Quilts

Ursula Michael

700 East State Street • Iola, WI 54990-0001
715-445-2214 • 888-457-2873
www.krausebooks.com

Our toll-free number to place an order or obtain a free catalog is (800) 258-0929.

The following registered trademark terms and companies appear in this publication: Airtex®, Glue Dots™, HeatnBond®, Sulky®, The Warm™ Company's Steam-A-Seam®, Prismacolor®.

Library of Congress Control Number: 2007923006

ISBN-13: 978-0-89689-539-3
ISBN-10: 0-89689-539-4

Designed by Heidi Bittner-Zastrow
Edited by Tracy L. Conradt

Printed in China

Dedication

This book is dedicated to my husband and best friend, Al, who has given me the freedom and support to pursue my creative projects for over 25 years.

Acknowledgments

A book requires the assistance of many hard-working people. Thanks to my editor, Tracy Conradt, for her opinions, suggestions and miracles she worked to help me create this book. Thanks to my photographer, book designers and the team at Krause for making my work look good. Thanks to FreeSpirit, Sullivan's, Starr Designs and Bali Fabrics for supplying many of the fabrics needed to make these quilts. Thanks to Airtex for the batting; Wonderfil, YLI and Sulky for thread; to Kreinik for the metallic braid; and Misty Fuse, HeatnBond and The Warm Company's Steam-a-Seam for the fusible adhesives. It has been my pleasure to work with such lovely people and quality products.

Contents

Introduction

When I was a child I loved to play paper dolls. I would spend hours drawing the dolls and creating all kinds of outfits to dress them. Then I would open up large paper bags and draw homes with rooms and furniture for the dolls to live in. This was my favorite rainy day activity. As I was working on the projects for this book, the same creative feelings flowed back to me. Drawing the appliqué motifs, sorting through my fabrics and arranging them on the blocks reprised such familiar feelings that I had to laugh at myself. What a great way to spend a rainy day even now!

Soon after I got married, I discovered quilting as a hobby. By day I worked as a graphic artist and in the evenings I quilted. It was not too long before I discovered that I could make quilts and sell my patterns. As I entered the world of needle arts, quilting, crochet and cross stitch design gradually took over my life, and for 25 years I have enjoyed a wonderful career of designing with fabrics and fibers.

Pieced quilts have a rhythm, often a repetitive pattern that is relaxing, and once established it can be worked for days. Appliqué quilts that were once stitched by hand also developed a rhythm as each motif was carefully applied to a background. Today's appliqué quilts have the option of quick fusing, machine quilting and speedy finishing techniques, which are well-suited to busy lifestyles. Like the difference in listening to smooth jazz versus funky jazz, you have a choice to quilt in your own rhythm.

I love color. I love fabric. I love to be surrounded by things that make me feel good. Fabric shopping takes me hours as I select prints and colors that please me, arranging them in my carriage like flowers in a vase. Having the stash of fat quarters, batiks and prints stacked on my shelves makes me feel prepared when the inspiration hits. The 27 projects shown are quick to finish, perhaps on a rainy day when you get the sudden urge to quilt. Some motifs are simple one-color appliqués; others require a selection of fabrics. My models were made with bright colors that appeal to me. Feel free to alter the colors to ones that you prefer, ones that make you feel good.

"What I make with my hands,
I give with my heart."

Ursula Michael

General Instructions

Once you discover how easy fusible appliqué quilting is you'll be making quilts for every occasion. Take a few minutes to read through these basic instructions before beginning a project. The individual project instructions are brief and focus on color selection and layout. The "how to" general instructions apply to every project and give a more detailed explanation of all the steps needed to complete the project.

Finished Size

This is the total size of the quilt including borders and binding.

Making a Project Larger or Smaller

Most appliqué designs can be made into larger wall hangings, outdoor flags or bed quilts. They can be used on smaller table linens, adorn wearables or on tote bags. If you want to change the size of the appliqué motif, bring the pattern to a copy center and have them enlarge or reduce the pattern for you, or print it off your own printer at a reduced size. Another way to enlarge the project is to make multiple blocks of the same design or add several borders. Remember to purchase extra yardage to complete your quilt. Use the appliqué motifs as a starting point to create your own rainy day project.

Materials (fat quarters)

When you see "fat quarters" immediately following the materials caption, any fabric suggestions listed that do not have a specific yardage requirement will use fat quarters. A fat quarter is a piece of fabric cut approximately 18" x 22", one quarter of a one-yard piece of fabric. A typical running quarter yard cut of fabric is 9" x 44". The fat quarter cut is more suitable for piecing and appliqué of small quilts. Since many of the appliqué quilts use small amounts of fabric, you probably won't need to purchase every color. Check out your stash of fabrics and supplement what you already have. It's okay to make the color changes! It's your quilt. If you like blue, go ahead and change a yellow background to blue. The color suggestions are what were used in the model quilts.

Choosing Fabric

Selecting fabric for your quilt is a lot like putting together an outfit. I pull out my bins of fabric and pick out a few colors that I'd like to use for my background and borders. Next I start pulling out fabrics for the appliqué motifs, mixing and matching until I have a blend of colors that pleases me. If you look closely at the fabric used in the quilts, you will see that batiks are used most often. Batiks have subtle color changes that give dimension to the appliqué shapes. Solid colors tend to look flat and primitive. Using small prints can enhance a design. For example, mittens and hats will have a knitted look with a textured print, snowmen sparkle with white-on-white prints, and kittens look great in a furry print. As a general rule, when in doubt, choose a batik.

Many of the background blocks are light values. Value is the lightness or darkness of a color, not the color itself. Working on a light-colored background makes the color selection for the motifs much easier than working on a dark- or medium-value background. In the suggested colors list, the value of the colors is divided into very light, light, medium, dark and very dark. This gives five values of a color to choose from. When organizing your colors, you might find a medium green will blend in too much with a medium blue. Simply changing the medium green to a light green can alter the whole fabric composition. Taking a little extra time here to play with your fabric colors will make your final quilt sparkle.

Preparation

For fusible small quilts, I never pre-wash the fabric. Washing seems to take out some of the stiffness that I like in new fabric. I press the wrinkles and folds out of the fabric before fusing. I also consider the mini quilts as easy home décor created to give almost instant pleasure. Unlike heirloom bed quilts which should use pre-washed fabrics, my mini quilts are made more like an art or craft project.

All About Fusible Products

All of the projects in this book have appliqué designs that are fused to the background fabric. I believe that quick and easy appliqué should be just that ... quick and easy. There is an assortment of fusible adhesive products available in the market today. For the best results, first determine what the end use of the quilted item will be. If it is a seasonal wall quilt with minimal quilting, a paper-backed extra hold adhesive that enables you to trace the design on the paper will make your work go quickly. For a mini quilt that will be enhanced with more all-over machine quilting, you'll want to use a fusible adhesive that allows easier machine stitching. An adhesive that boasts ultra hold strength will permanently hold the appliqué shapes to the background without additional quilting. Some fusible adhesives lightly secure the fabric to the background like a basting stitch, and require quilting or top stitching to keep them in place. There's no right or wrong choice, and I imagine in a few years there will be even more fusible choices. Your best bet is to experiment with various fusibles by making small samples to see how they work and what feels like the right choice for your project.

Fusible appliqué has some unique qualities, one of them being raw edges. Since my small quilt projects are made just for fun, this does not bother me. I love to make these quilts in a day and display them in the evening. The appliqué edges can be secured by machine stitching with invisible monofilament thread, or with a fine zigzag stitch in thread that matches the fabric. This stitching seems like a lot of extra work for me, so I just skip this step and make sure that the fusible product I use holds the fabric together securely. If seeing raw edges does not agree with you, feel free to turn the edges under as in traditional quilting. Remember to add a seam allowance when cutting the appliqué shapes.

Fusible appliqué also has a flat, clean look, which is fine with me. When selecting fabric,

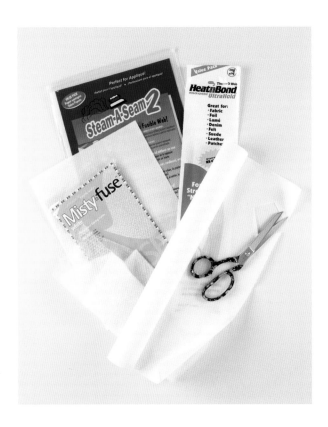

batiks have a dimensional light and dark quality. Strong primary colors that are opposite on the color wheel make your quilts twinkle. Color value is also important to consider when laying out your design. Some free motion quilting to hold the layers together will add texture to the surface, too. Just because the fabric is fused, the quilt needs not to appear flat.

How to Fuse

The first step is to read the manufacturer's instructions. Every fusible adhesive product is used a little differently, from transferring the design, to the temperature setting of the iron. I have found the paper-backed fusible adhesive is the easiest to use. HeatnBond Iron-On Adhesive and Steam-A-Seam Double Stick Fusible Web offer several kinds of paper-backed products. Some adhesives are used as a temporary hold for the fabric; some ultra hold products offer a permanent bond. The products come as a sheet of slick paper with a layer of heat sensitive plastic webbing on one side.

The design elements are traced on the side of the paper with no adhesive or webbing. Place the design under the paper backed adhesive sheet on a light box or tape both sheets to a window so you can see the pattern. It is very important to remember that the finished motif will be reversed when you trace it. If you need to reverse the motif, flip the pattern to the back side and trace. Leave about ½" between the shapes to allow for cutting.

Place the pattern on the back side of your fabric and iron on. Most adhesives require a low temperature setting for this first step. Too much heat may melt all of the plastic into the fabric and not allow it to stick to the background.

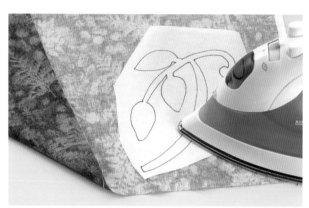

Cut your pattern pieces on your drawing lines.

Peel off the paper exposing the adhesive and arrange the pattern pieces, adhesive side down on your background fabric.

When the pattern pieces are ironed with a high temperature, the adhesive sticks them together.

Tip

Why I like to Fuse:

Fusing is fast. I can cut, arrange and fuse my quilt top in less than an hour.

Fusing is not fussy. There's no precise hand sewing and worrying about turning corners, making points and lumpy seams.

Fusing is easy. It's like a cut and paste scrapbook project.

Fusing is forgiving. If the appliqué shapes don't exactly align, it's OK.

Misty Fuse is a very light web without a paper backing. This product is placed on the back side of your fabric and sandwiched between sheets of parchment paper. Press to lightly apply the fuse to fabric. Peel back one of the parchment papers. The appliqué pattern can be transferred to the remaining parchment. Layer the adhesive side down on your fabric, lightly iron on. Trim the pattern pieces, remove the paper and arrange on the background. Use a dry hot iron to permanently fuse. This particular adhesive webbing is lovely to use for heavy quilting.

Other fusible products include fusible tape that can be applied to the edges of the pattern to temporarily hold them until quilting. This is great for use when you have straight lines. Temporary fabric glue may also be used to hold down the pattern pieces until they are quilted. Transfer paper will come in handy when using certain fusible products.

A non-stick pressing sheet can help you arrange an appliqué design that has many pieces. Prepare your pattern pieces using your favorite fusible product. Working on an ironing board, place the pressing sheet on top of the illustration. You should be able to see the line drawing through the pressing sheet. Arrange the pattern pieces on the pressing sheet. Fuse the pieces together with your iron set at the coolest setting possible—just warm enough to hold the unit together. Let the fused unit cool and peel it off the pressing sheet. It is now ready to apply to your background fabric.

These how-to instructions for fusing are general and should be tweaked as needed for each project. I can't stress enough the importance of reading the manufacturer's instructions before you begin using the fusible adhesive. Every product is heat sensitive and works best as advised.

Two-Sided Appliqué

The dangling hearts in My Dancing Hearts, page 116, are two layers of fabric fused together. Extra hold fusible adhesive must be used for this technique. Iron the fusible pattern paper on the wrong side of your fabric.

Trim the excess fabric around the heart.

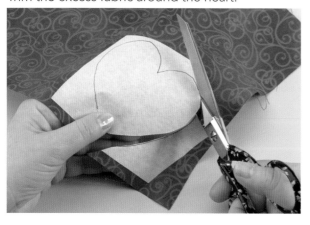

Peel off the paper backing.

Iron the heart appliqué to the wrong side of another fabric piece.

Trim the excess fabric around the heart.

Your completed heart will be a two-sided piece.

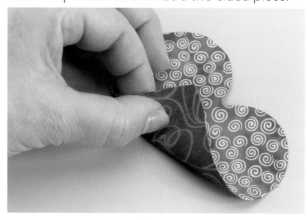

Tip

When you have completed making the two sided appliqué, you can shape and bend the appliqué while it is still warm. Hold in place until the appliqué cools down. It will permanently retain the shape. If you want to change or flatten the appliqué, press again and work with it when it is warm.

Piecing

Unlike traditional quilts, my small quilts are entirely pieced before the appliqué motifs are fused for several reasons. Once pieced, you can see how the colors of the appliqué motifs look against the background and borders. If the motifs seem to fade or the colors look awkward together, you can easily replace the fabric with another color. Centering the appliqué is easier once the borders are added. I even add the final binding or border at the same time. Machine stitching everything at one sitting seems to make the project roll along faster.

Always use quarter-inch seams when piecing the blocks and borders.

EZBorders

Measuring, cutting and sewing exact borders takes time and energy. I prefer to make a long continuous border and trim it as I sew it to the quilt blocks. Use a rotary cutter for cutting quick and accurate border strips.

Place the fabric on the cutting mat, aligning the raw edge with the measured lines on the board. Align the ruler on the desired width of the border strip and cut as many strips as needed for your length. Sew the lengths end to end. The material lists give a total number of inches plus a few extra inches for insurance.

Starting at one end of the long strip, place the border strip along the raw edge of your block right sides together. Do not trim the long end of the border strip. Sew the border to the side of your block. Now you can trim the tail end of the border strip even with the bottom edge of the block. You've just completed the first EZBorder! Continue by sewing another border strip to the opposite side of the block.

Place your next border strip on the top edge of your block right sides together, aligning the border strip with the new block corners. Sew in place. Repeat on the bottom side of the block.

Additional borders and bindings are added in the same EZBorder manner.

This same method may be used to make log cabin style borders or bias cut borders.

Pressing

After your quilt top is pieced and appliquéd, iron the back side, folding the seams toward the darker color fabric. Flip the quilt to the front and iron the appliqués and borders by gently lifting and pressing the iron. Try not to glide the iron over the fused shapes because the hot iron may lift some edges that were not adhered thoroughly.

Batting

Batting for fusible wall and table quilts should be thin and light-weight. Since we're doing minimal quilting, a thick batting would produce large lumps in the unquilted areas and shrink the fabric in the quilted areas, causing your quilt to look misshapen and hang unevenly. I have used an 80/20 Cotton Poly blend from Airtex that gives just enough loft and body to accent the quilting lines.

Quilt Basting

Since I discovered quilt basting spray, I have never thread basted my quilt layers together again. A light mist of this tacky spray will temporarily hold your layers together before you quilt. The basting spray label advises you to use it in a ventilated area, and it is flammable, so take the required precautions.

After your quilt top is finished and pressed, layer batting and backing on the back side of the quilt top. Lift one half of the backing to expose the batting, and lightly mist the batting. Fold the

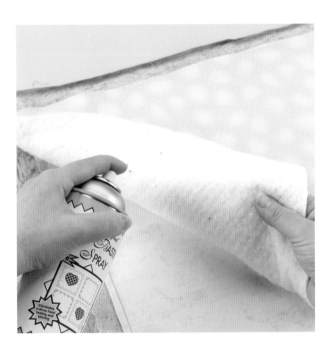

backing back in place. Repeat on the other side. Smooth the backing with your hands. Flip the quilt and repeat with the quilt top. The spray will remain sticky for several weeks. This basting spray holds the layers nicely and there's no danger of pinpricks when manipulating the fabric in machine quilting.

Another way to fuse baste your quilt is to use up your fusible scraps. Remove the paper backing and scatter leftover pieces of the fusible adhesive on the batting spacing them a few inches apart. You won't need to completely cover the quilt to keep the layers sticking together. Layer the top and backing to the batting, and iron to hold the layers together.

Thread

There's a rainbow of colors and varieties of thread to choose for quilting. Cotton, polyester and rayon threads are terrific choices to enhance your quilt. To quilt easily through the fusible adhesive, I prefer a fine monofilament thread in both the needle and bobbin. This is the only thread that does not break for me when I stitch through any adhesive product. Monofilament thread also disappears into the background and the motifs seem to pop out nicely. The lightweight adhesives accept more kinds of thread than the ultra hold adhesives, causing less breakage as you quilt. Make a test sample and practice to see what works for your particular fabric.

Stitching

Do a little machine stitching to make sure your machine is set up properly. Fuse a few fabric scraps to a background, and layer a piece of batting and backing. Quick spray with basting spray. Use a new needle in your machine. Thread your bobbin with the thread you will use for quilting. As you practice a quilting stitch, check the tension and adjust both the top and bottom settings. I like to drop my feed dogs when quilting curvy lines to give me more control. When quilting borders in the ditch, I prefer to keep the feed dogs up. Become one with your machine to make your quilting flow.

Quilting

My approach to quilting is also quick and easy. Sitting at a machine for hours seems like work to me, so my quilts have minimal quilting. Some of the quilts are only stitched in the ditch on the borders and around the appliqué motifs. If I'm in a mood for more quilting, I do free form quilting. In my opinion, pieced quilts seem to look nicer in an all over quilting pattern. Appliqué quilts have a central design or several motifs that are focal points, so quilting around them "frames" the pictures. Whatever works for you is the right way.

Quilting Tips

Start quilting in the middle of your quilt and work out towards the side edges.

Draw your free form motif on paper first to train your brain to visualize the motif as you quilt.

Long straight lines are tedious to keep straight, so add curves on purpose.

It is OK to let quilting lines cross.

Run your quilting lines up to the final border, or about 1½" from the raw edges of the top to allow for turning the edge to the back side to finish.

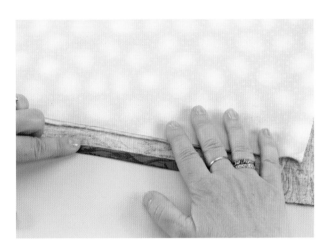

Finishing

After your quilting is complete, it's time to finish the edges. This is my favorite way to finish. Place the quilt face down on the table. Carefully trim the excess batting and backing, leaving about 1" of the quilt top available for turning.

Fold back the binding, tucking under ¼" for the hem.

Pin the edges to the backing and hand sew the seam with a tiny slip stitch.

To make neat corners, trim one binding even with the end of the block. Tuck the short edge of the binding on the next side under ¼" (trimming if needed). Fold back the binding, tucking under ¼" as before, for the hem. Slip stitch in place.

To finish in a no sew method, trim the batting and backing as indicated above. Apply fusible tape to the edge of the 1" seam on the back side of the quilt binding. Fold the hem back flat, pin in place and iron the fusible tape to the back of the quilt.

Label Your Quilt

Now that your project is complete, make a name label to add to the back of your quilt. A label should contain the following information:

Title of the quilt
Quilt maker's name
Date
Quilt recipient
Special occasion, if any

Computer printer fabric is an awesome way to get this done quickly. Design the labels on the computer; insert the special paper-backed fabric into your inkjet printer, and print. Allow the ink to dry. Apply fusible adhesive to back side of the label, trim and iron on to the back of the quilt.

Tip

To make a really special label, use your digital camera to take a photo of an appliqué block. Transfer the motif into almost any word or design type of program. Size the motif to about 1" and add the quilt information as text placed to the side of the motif. Print your label and fuse to the back of your quilt.

Sleeve Hanger

A simple sleeve to hang your quilt is made from a 6"-wide strip of fabric. Measure and cut the strip the width of your finished quilt. Apply fusible tape to the top and bottom lengthwise edges of the strip. Align the strip about ½" from the top edge on the back of your quilt. Press in place. Alternately, the sleeve may be hand basted to the back of your quilt.

Tools and Notions

You will find the following supplies helpful for fusible appliqué quilting:

A large flat surface with good lighting

Sewing machine in good working order

Light table

Iron and ironing board

Non-stick pressing sheet

Spray bottle filled with water

Dressmaker's shears

Embroidery scissors for snipping and cutting small shapes

Rotary cutter, rotary cutting mat, rotary ruler

Quilt pins and pincushion

Thimble

Quilter's glove

No. 2 pencil

Yardstick or ruler

Threads for machine sewing

Quilt basting spray

Colored pencils

Fish Tank

A tropical fish tank will make an exotic splash on your wall and there's no worry about feeding the fish! Richly colored batiks hold the key to making the fish and coral sparkle on the deep blue background.

Finished size: 26" x 26"

Materials

Fat quarters

Batting 28" x 28"

Backing 28" x 28"

Blue rayon thread for quilting

*Suggested colors:

The fish look best in an assortment of the brightest batiks you can find. (Starr Design Fabrics were used)

The water background is made from five different deep blue batiks. The thread used was Wonderfil Rayon, Mirage.

Refer to General Instructions on page 7 for assistance with basic sewing and quilting instruction.

Piecing

1 Sew the four background rectangles and center square together as shown on page 22.

2 Sew the orange borders to the dark blue borders lengthwise, trimming the ends even.

3 Sew a corner square to the end of a border strip.

4 Sew the border/corner strips to the large center using EZBorder method.

Appliqué

1 Prepare the appliqué shapes using your favorite fusible method.

2 Assemble the individual appliqué design pieces on the pieced background.

3 Press in place.

Fabric	Cut	For
4 dark blue batiks	4 rectangles 9" x 11½"	Background
4 rectangles	1 strip 3¾" x 80"	Outside border
Fifth blue batik	4 squares 4¾" x 4¾"	Corners of border
Dark blue batik	1 square 3" x 3"	Center square
Orange batik	1 strip ¾" x 80"	Inner border

Finishing

1 Layer the finished top, batting and backing.

2 Apply quilt basting spray.

3 This model was quilted with free form stitching around the fish and coral appliqués.

4 After quilting is complete, trim excess batting and backing.

5 Fold back the outer border and hand sew the edges to the back side to finish.

Tip

Quilting is a good thing to do when you feel your stress level rise.

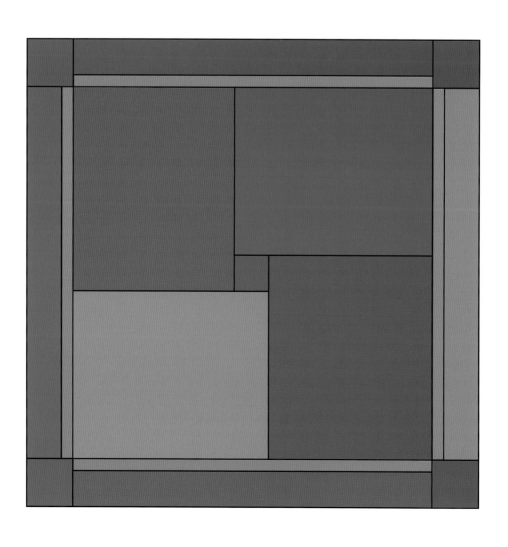

Sea Life

Create your own seaside memories with a sea life wall banner. Soft sky colors reflect in a shimmering watery background. Seashells and starfish float carelessly in a tidal pool and wash out to sea.

Finished size: 18½" x 29"

Materials

Suggested colors:

Fat quarter very light blue batik
  (background)

Fat quarter very light yellow, lavender
  and green (squares)

Fat quarter dark brown, gray and
  mauve (seashell motifs)

Fat quarter dark brown (inner border)

½ yd. light print outer border

½ yd. light print binding

Light blue rayon thread for quilting

Batting 20" x 31"

Backing 20" x 31"

Light blue thread for quilting
  (Sulky 100% Cotton was used)

Refer to General Instructions on page
7 for assistance with basic sewing and
quilting instruction.

Piecing

1 Sew inner border to the background using
EZBorder method.

2 Sew outer border using EZBorder method.

3 Sew binding using EZBorder method.

Appliqué

1 Prepare the appliqué shapes using your
favorite fusible method.

2 Assemble the individual design pieces on
the blue background.

3 Press in place.

Fabric	Cut	For
Very light blue batik	1 rectangle 13½" x 24"	Background
Dark brown	1 strip 1¼" x 76"	Inner border
Light print	1 strip 2" x 100"	Outer border
Light print	1 strip 1½" x 100"	Binding

Finishing

1 Layer the finished top, batting and backing.

2 Apply the quilt basting spray.

3 This model was quilted in free form lines over the entire quilt.

4 After quilting is complete, trim excess batting and backing.

5 Fold the binding back, and hand sew the edges to the back side to finish.

Tip

Value is the intensity of color, not the color itself. The stronger the contrast between the values in your fabric colors, the more vibrant your quilt will look. Colors that are similar in value blend softly together.

Scallop Festival Quilt

By repeating a simple appliqué scallop shell in the center section and an easy seaweed vine in the wide border area, this medallion quilt spins around like a playful carousel-by-the-sea. The opposite colors of blue and orange in pastel shades make the quilt glow like a heavenly sunset on a warm summer eve.

Finished size: 35" x 35"

Materials

Suggested colors:

Fat quarters of batiks for seashells, seaweed borders and starfish

Fat quarters of three shades of blue batik prints in a watery style used for the center square background

½ yd. dark blue inner border and binding

½ yd. peach wide border

Batting 37" x 37"

Backing 37" x 37"

Monofilament thread and peach colored variegated thread for quilting.

*This quilt was constructed with Princess Mirah Bali Fabrics

Refer to general Instructions on page 7 for assistance with basic sewing and quilting instructions.

Cutting

Cut blue background squares 12" x 12" each, one of one print, one of second print, two of third print.

Piecing

1 Arrange and sew one of each triangle of the "third print" to a "first" and "second" print.

2 Sew the four squares together, placing the "third" print on the outside of the large square.

3 Sew the dark blue inner EZBorder around the set of four squares.

4 Sew the peach EZBorder around the center section.

5 Sew the dark blue outer border around the center section.

Fabric	Cut	For
Watery blue	4 squares 12" x 12" then cut in half diagonally to make 8 triangles	Background
Dark blue	1 strip 1½" x 100"	Inner border
Dark blue	1 strip 2" x 150"	Binding
Peach	1 strip 4½" x 120"	Middle border

Assembly

1 Prepare the appliqué shapes using your favorite fusible method.

2 Assemble the individual design pieces on the center square and the wide border.

3 Press in place.

Finishing

1 Layer the finished top, batting and backing.

2 Apply quilt basting spray.

3 This model was quilted to enhance the scallop shells with the peach variegated thread. The remainder of the quilt was quilted with monofilament thread in a wavy pattern mimicking the seaweed appliqué motifs.

4 After quilting is complete, trim excess batting and backing.

5 Fold back the front outer border and hand sew the edges to the back side to finish.

Tip

Sometimes it's fun to think different when choosing fabric colors for appliqué. Balancing color and color values often gives the quilt more life than using conventional colors for appliqué motifs.

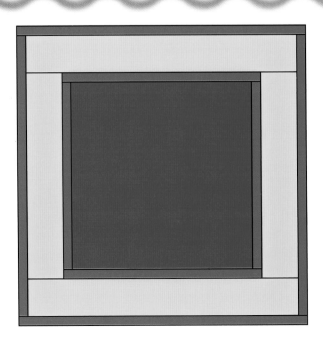

Rainy Day Umbrella

No need to dread a rainy day! It's a great time to take out your favorite fabrics and fuse together a terrific project that can be finished in one day, or a perhaps a snowy weekend.

Finished size: 12½" x 12½"

Materials

Suggested colors:

Fat quarters of brightly colored batiks
    in yellow, red and green

Light blue/pink batik (background)

Dark aqua (inner border)

Red (outer border)

Light blue glass seed beads, small
    amount

Red, green and yellow glass beads,
    ½" size, about 24 pieces

Bead thread and fine needle

½ yd. yellow ribbon

Batting 14" x 14"

Backing 14" x 14"

Monofilament thread for quilting

Refer to General Instructions on page
7 for assistance with basic sewing and
quilting instruction.

Piecing

1 Sew the two borders, right sides together, lengthwise.

2 Align the border unit on the right side of the block right sides together.

3 Sew together and trim the excess border length leaving a 3" tail at the bottom.

4 Align a border unit with the top side of the block, right sides together. Sew and trim evenly.

5 Repeat on left and bottom sides.

6 Sew the tail of the right side border to the bottom border.

Assembly

1 Prepare the appliqué shapes using your favorite fusible method.

2 Assemble the individual design pieces.

3 Press in place.

Fabric	Cut	For
Dark aqua	1 strip 1" x 48"	Inner border
Red	1 strip 2½" x 48"	Outer border
Light blue/pink batik	1 square 10½" x 10½"	Background

Finishing

1 Layer the finished top, batting and backing.

2 Apply quilt basting spray.

3 This model was quilted in the ditch on the borders and around the umbrella motif.

4 After quilting is complete, trim excess batting and backing.

5 Fold back the binding and hand sew the edges to the back side to finish.

Embellish

1 Use a bead needle and thread to secure a few seeds beads in diagonal rows on the background to suggest raindrops.

2 To make the dangle beads at the bottom of the umbrella, secure the thread at one end of the umbrella. Thread a large bead and a small bead, run the needle back into the large bead using the small bead to secure the large bead. Make a stitch or two into the fabric with the thread and repeat anchoring the beads along the edge of the umbrella. Space the beads evenly and alternate the colors. Secure the thread at the end.

3 Cut ribbon in half and make two bows. Secure to the top left and right corners of the quilt.

Tip

If you like a particular design motif, multiply it and enlarge it to use in individual blocks and make a full-size quilt.

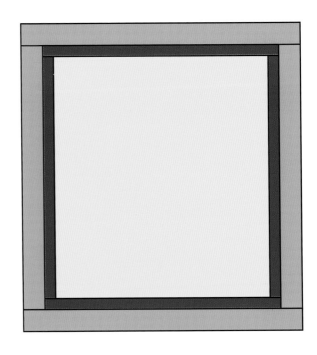

Umbrella Dance

When it rains, the umbrellas come out to dance! Bobbing up and down, in and out under the raindrops, they parade like flowers on a line dance. What a delightful spark on a dreary rainy day.

Finished size: 19½" x 22"

Materials

Suggested colors:

Fat quarter of batik pastel fabric
    for background

Fat quarters of red, dark green and
    pink for umbrella #1

Fat quarters of lime green, orange and
    lemon for umbrella #2

Fat quarters of dark blue, teal and lime
    green for umbrella #3

Scrap of turquoise blue for raindrops

Fat quarter of dark blue (inner border)

Fat quarter of medium red (outer
    border)

Fat quarter of dotted print for binding

Batting 21½" x 24"

Backing 21½" x 24"

Monofilament thread for quilting

Refer to General Instructions on page
7 for assistance with basic sewing and
quilting instruction.

Piecing

1 Sew dark blue inner border using EZBorder method.

2 Sew red border using EZBorder method.

3 Sew print binding using EZBorder method.

Appliqué

1 Prepare the appliqué shapes using your favorite fusible method.

2 Assemble the individual design pieces on the background.

3 Press in place.

Fabric	Cut	For
Pastel batik	1 rectangle 14½" x 17½"	Background
Dark blue	1 strip 1¼" x 70"	Inner border
Red	1 strip 2" x 76"	Outer border
Print	1 strip 1" x 80"	Binding

Finishing

1 Layer the finished top, batting and backing.

2 Apply the quilt basting spray.

3 This model was quilted in diagonal raindrop lines over the entire quilt.

4 After quilting is complete, trim excess batting and backing.

5 Fold the binding back, and hand sew the edges to the back side to finish.

Tip

When you have lots of small similar appliqué pieces, numbering them before you cut them out will help you keep them in order. My system is to use a letter for the color and a number for the placement of the piece. For example "R3" would be red fabric and the third appliqué piece from the left on my pattern. The entire pattern is coded first. As I trace each of the shapes on the paper backed adhesive I write the code for it right on the shape.

Butterfly Window

When the evening draws near and the sky softens,
notice how the butterflies flicker in and out of the shadows.

Finished size: 28" x 28"

Materials

Suggested colors:

Fat quarters bright orange, blue, green, purple for the butterflies

½ yd. navy blue for the filigree design and binding

½ yd. batik light yellow/orange for five background blocks

Fat quarter batik light blue for four background blocks

Fat quarter batik light blue/orange blend for the border

Batting 30" x 30"

Backing 30" x 30"

Sunset colored thread for quilting (Sulky 100% Cotton was used)

Refer to General Instructions on page 7 for assistance with basic sewing and quilting instruction.

Piecing

1 Sew a light yellow/orange rectangle to each side of the center block matching lengths. Refer to the quilt diagram on page 42.

2 Sew a light blue square to each short side of the top rectangle. Repeat for the bottom row.

3 Sew the top and bottom units to the center unit to form a large square.

4 Sew the blue/orange blend border around the square using EZBorder method.

5 Sew the navy binding using EZBorder method.

Appliqué

1 Prepare the appliqué shapes using your favorite fusible method. Cut 4 small heart corner motifs and 24 larger heart motifs.

2 Assemble each butterfly as one unit.

3 Arrange the corner motifs and the butterfly units on the background squares. The smaller heart motif is used only in the four outer corners.

4 Press in place.

Fabric	Cut	For
Light yellow/orange	4 rectangles 8" x 10½"	Background blocks
	1 square 10½" x 10½"	Background center block
Light blue	4 squares 8" x 8"	Background corner blocks
Light blue/orange	1 strip 1½" x 116"	Border
Navy blue	1 strip 2" x 120"	Binding

Finishing

1 Layer the finished top, batting and backing.

2 Apply quilt basting spray.

3 After quilting is complete, fold back the navy blue border and hand sew to the back side to finish.

4 This model is quilted with lines around the butterflies and a free form line inside the filigree motifs. The border has a decorative vine quilting pattern.

Tip

Use fabric colors with a high contrast to make your quilt sparkle. Notice how the background colors in the Butterfly Window quilt are all the same light value and blend together. The butterflies and heart motifs are dark values of the same colors used in the background. A great way to see value is to put your fabrics against a wall, step back across the room and look at your quilt. Make sure you can see the edges of the appliqué shapes clearly.

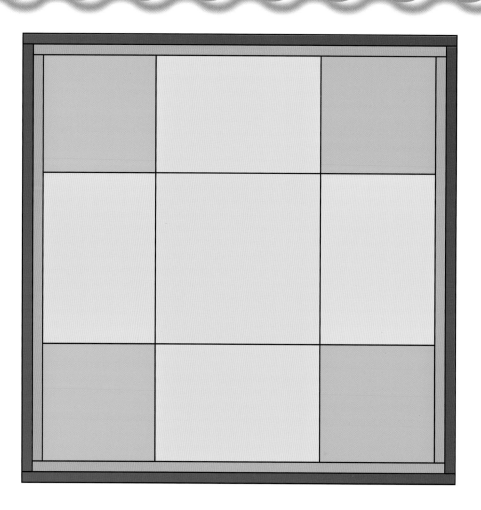

Four Seasons

Choose some brightly colored fabrics to make a seasonal quilt to cheer up a back door entryway.

Finished size 23" x 23"

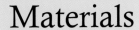

Materials

Use fat quarters unless otherwise stated

Pieced background

½ yd. lime green

½ yd. medium green

Spring

Fuchsia (background)

Yellow, orange and pink (with blue)
  flowers

Dark green and lime leaves

Summer

Yellow (background)

Two shades of red for the cherries

Medium green, lime and dark green
  for leaves

Fall

Medium brown (background)

Two shades of orange for the pumpkin

Lime for the leaves

Dark green for the stem

Winter

Dark blue background

White snowflake

Center block

Medium green (background)

Yellow for the heart

Side triangles

Dark blue, medium brown, fuchsia and
  yellow

Medium green for binding, cut 2" x 100"

Medium green backing, cut 25" x 25"

Batting 25" x 25"

Green thread for quilting
  (Sulky 100% Cotton was used)

This quilt has five blocks set on an angle.
The four seasonal blocks use medium
green borders and the center block
uses a lime border. The side triangles
use lime borders. All of the borders are
stitched using the EZBorder method.

Refer to General Instructions on page
7 for assistance with basic sewing and
quilting instruction.

Fabric	Cut	For
Medium green	4 strips 1¾" x 28"	Seasons border
Lime	1 strip 1¾" x 28"	Center block border
Lime	4 strips 1¾" x 18"	Half blocks borders
Lime	1 square 9" x 9" cut in four triangles	Corner triangles
Fuchsia	1 square 5½" x 5½"	Background spring block
Yellow	1 square 5½" x 5½"	Background summer block
Medium brown	1 square 5½" x 5½"	Background fall block
Dark blue	1 square 5½" x 5½"	Background winter block
Medium green	1 square 5½" x 5½"	Background center block
Fuchsia	1 right triangle 6" x 6" x 8½"	Center side triangle
Yellow	1 right triangle 6" x 6" x 8½"	Center side triangle
Medium brown	1 right triangle 6" x 6" x 8½"	Center side triangle
Dark blue	1 right triangle 6" x 6" x 8½"	Center side triangle

Piecing

1 Sew the lime border to the medium green 5½" x 5½" square in a log cabin style.

2 Sew the medium green borders to the remaining four squares in a log cabin style.

3 Sew the lime borders to the four side triangles log cabin style. Trim ends.

4 Place the spring block, center block and the winter block in a row. Sew together.

5 Place the medium brown triangle, summer block and fuchsia triangle in a row. Sew together.

6 Place the dark blue triangle, fall block and yellow triangle in a row and sew together.

7 Align the three rows. Sew together.

8 Sew the corner squares to the set of blocks to form a large square quilt.

9 Sew the outer border strips using EZBorder method.

Appliqué

1 Prepare the appliqué motifs using your favorite fusible method.

2 Assemble the individual design pieces on the pieced background quilt.

3 Press in place.

Finishing

1 Layer the finished front, batting and backing.

2 Apply quilt basting spray between the layers.

3 This model was quilted in a free form vine motif that meanders on the borders.

4 After quilting is complete, fold back the medium green border and hand sew to the back side to finish the edges.

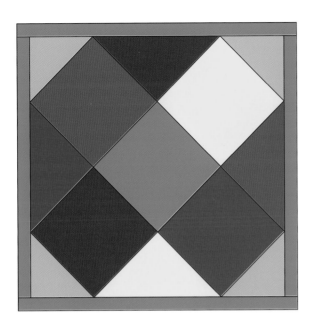

Tip

Replace rotary cutter blades often. If the blade can't cut through the fabric in one smooth motion, replace it. Mats wear out too. If you're having trouble cutting with a new blade, your mat may need to be replaced.

Heart Maze

See how one delicate heart motif creates a lacy pattern on square blocks.
The cutting of the motifs may take some time, but fusing takes just minutes.

Finished size: 31" x 31"

Materials

½ yd. each of four textured prints for
background blocks*

½ yd. each of four darker values of
background blocks for heart motifs*

½ yd. additional of one of the heart
motif fabrics for binding**

Batting 33" x 33"

Backing 33" x 33"

Monofilament thread for quilting

*I used four similar in value fabrics that
are the same textured print for my
background blocks. The heart motifs
are four darker versions of the same
colors. You will need ½ yard of each
fabric.

**The bias cut binding uses one of the
darker colors, blue in this quilt, for an
additional ½ yard.

Refer to General Instructions on page
7 for assistance with basic sewing and
quilting instruction.

Piecing

1 Arrange the blocks as shown. Sew the rows.

2 Sew the row units together to form a large square.

3 To make the corner curves, use an 8" plate as a template to trace the cutting line. Trim excess corner fabric.

Appliqué

1 Prepare the appliqué shapes using your favorite fusible method.

2 Assemble the individual design pieces on the background blocks.

3 Press in place.

Fabric	Cut	For
Background fabric	4 squares 8" x 8" from each color	Background blocks
Binding	1 strip 2" x 144" bias cut	Binding

Finishing

1 Layer the finished top, batting and backing.

2 Apply the quilt basting spray.

3 This model was quilted in random swirly lines over the entire quilt.

4 After quilting is complete, trim excess batting and backing.

5 Sew the bias binding to the quilt right sides together, matching the raw edges.

6 Fold the binding back, and hand sew to the back side to finish the edges.

Tip

This motif would make an awesome border on a large quilt. The heart can be set on its point, placed on its side or alternated on left and right sides.

Welcome Kittens

We love to come home to a warm and fuzzy companion who tells you about his day by rubbing and purring (or barking!) This design is a great place to use animal prints or textures resembling fur and fuzz.

Finished size: 14½" x 35"

Materials

Suggested colors:

Fat quarters of assorted animal prints
    for the cats

Fat quarter gold plaid for the blocks

Fat quarters of several dark brown
    prints for the box outlines and letters

½ yd. light gold (background)

⅛ yd. black (inner border)

Fat quarter print (outer border)

Backing 16" x 37"

Batting 16" x 37"

Monofilament thread for quilting

Refer to General Instructions on page
7 for assistance with basic sewing and
quilting instruction.

Piecing

1 Sew the black inner border using EZBorder
method.

2 Sew the outer print border using EZBorder
method.

Appliqué

1 Prepare the appliqué shapes using your
favorite fusible method.

2 Assemble the individual design pieces on
the gold background.

3 Press in place.

Fabric	Cut	For
Light gold	1 rectangle 11" x 31"	Background
Black	1 strip 1" x 90"	Inner border
Animal print	1 strip 2½" x 98"	Outer border
Backing	1 rectangle 16" x 37"	Backing

Quilting

1 Layer the finished quilt top, batting and backing.

2 Apply quilt basting spray.

3 This model has outline quilting around the cats and blocks and in the ditch on the borders.

4 After quilting is complete, trim excess batting and backing.

5 Fold back the outer border, and hand sew the edges to the back side to finish.

Tip

The only time I like to hand sew is in the evening watching a good movie on TV. I get comfortable in my chair, arrange my sewing notions next to me and turn on a good light. Every one of my bindings is completed this way.

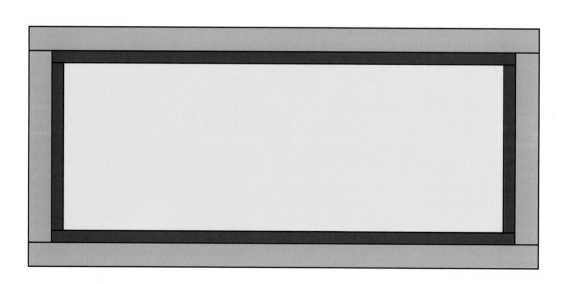

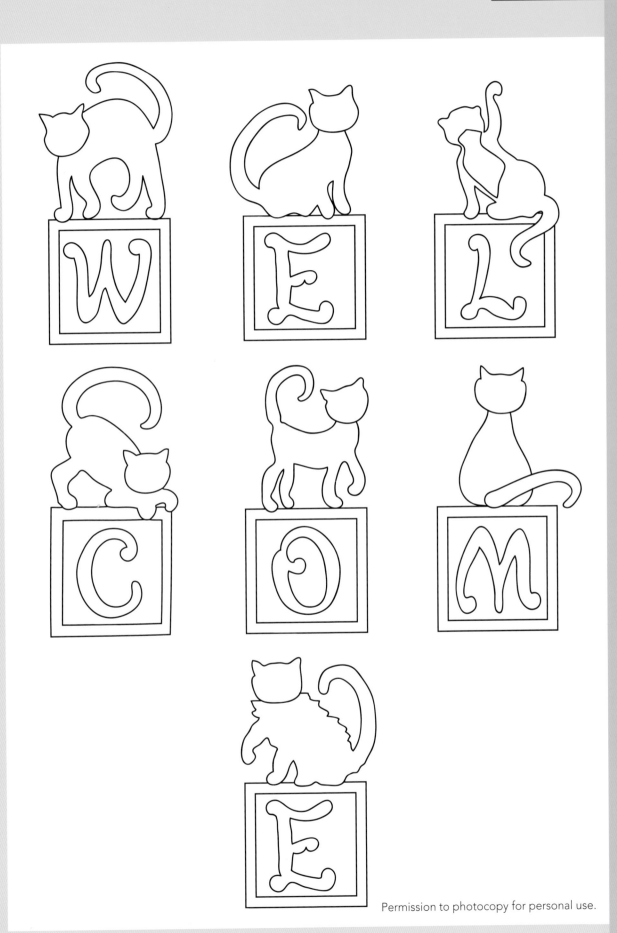

Happy Hour

Sometimes a rainy day calls for an evening happy hour.
If you have a special occasion to get together with friends, this banner is just for you!

Finished size: 11" x 43½"

Materials

Suggested colors:

Fat quarters of assorted "bubbly"
   prints

Fat quarter of black for rectangles

½ yd. gold dotted print

Fat quarter black print (border)

Fat quarter gold print (border)

Backing 13" x 45"

Batting 13" x 45"

Monofilament thread for quilting

Refer to General Instructions on page 7 for assistance with basic sewing and quilting instruction.

Appliqué

1 Prepare the appliqué shapes using your favorite fusible method.

2 Assemble the individual design pieces on black rectangles cut approximately ¾" larger than the motifs.

3 The black rectangles are placed slightly askew on print rectangles. The print rectangles are cut 9" tall and the width varies slightly (because each drink glass is a different size). Cut the rectangle 6" wide, and trim the width if needed. A gold print rectangle is alternated with three other fairly dark prints.

Piecing

1 Sew the row of blocks together.

2 Sew the inner black print border around the blocks using EZBorder method.

3 Sew the outer gold print border using EZBorder method.

Fabric	Cut	For
Black print	1 strip 1" x 102"	Inner border
Gold print	1 strip 2" x 114"	Outer border

Finishing

1 Layer the finished top, batting and backing.

2 Apply quilt basting spray.

3 This model was quilted in an all-over free form style.

4 After quilting is complete, fold back the outer border and hand sew the edges to the back side to finish.

Tip

The inspiration for this design came from a collection of "dotted" fabrics that I pulled out from my stash. The dots reminded me of bubbly drinks. How many dotted fabrics do you have in your closet?

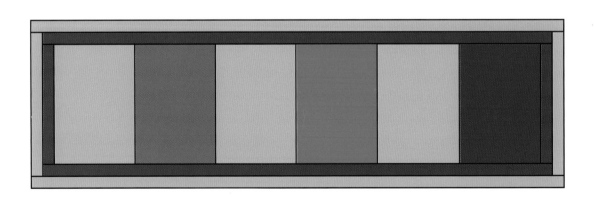

Redwork Place Mats

Whip up easy place mats to match any set of dishes or for a special occasion. Inspired by traditional redwork, a simple floral motif placed on a solid background sets off your table. If you like the clean look of the motifs, you can make a terrific mini quilt using just the motifs and placing the squares on a diagonal.

Finished size: 17" x 11" each

Materials

For one place mat:

Fat quarter white for background

Fat quarter dark colored solid, batik or print for the appliqué and borders

Fat quarter matching print for the stripes

Batting 19" x 13"

Backing 19" x 13"

Monofilament thread for quilting

Refer to General Instructions on page 7 for assistance with basic sewing and quilting instruction.

Assembly

1 Prepare the appliqué shapes using your favorite fusible method.

2 Arrange the motif on the background square.

3 Press in place.

Fabric	Cut	For
White	1 square 9" x 9"	Background
	1 strip 1¾" x 20"	Stripe
Matching print	1 strip 1⅝" x 15"	Stripe
Dark colored solid, batik or print	1 strip 1¾" x 66"	Borders

Piecing

1 Cut the white and solid strips into 5" lengths. Sew together, alternating colors.

2 Sew a border to each side of the striped unit.

3 Sew the appliquéd block to the unit. Sew the final side border to the block.

4 Sew a border to the top and bottom edges using EZBorder method.

5 Press finished top.

6 Layer the backing over the finished top, right sides together.

7 Machine sew around all the sides leaving a 5" opening for turning.

8 Clip corners. Turn right-side out. Press.

9 Trim batting to fit. Insert the batting inside the place mat. Hand sew the opening closed.

10 Quilt in the ditch around the white motif block and pieced striped rectangle.

Tip

These floral motifs would make a beautiful one color quilt! Cut as many motifs as needed to make a full-size quilt and border it with a matching toile print.

Coral Pillows

Sometimes a design is inspired by a special fabric. The free-form shapes of coral will showcase lovely batik prints. Choose colors in the same family as shown in the blue pillow, opposite colors shown on the rust and navy pillow, or two colors and black as on the gold pillow.

Finished size: 14" x 14" pillow

Materials

Suggested colors:

For one pillow:

Fat quarter batik print

Fat quarter light colored batik

Fat quarter dark colored batik

Backing, 2 pieces 14½" x 10"

14" pillow form

(Princess Mirah Bali fabrics were used)

Refer to General Instructions on page 7 for assistance with basic sewing and quilting instruction.

Appliqué

1 Prepare the appliqué shapes using your favorite fusible method.

2 Arrange the appliqué shapes on the background square.

3 Press in place.

Piecing

1 Sew the inner border to the background square using EZBorder method.

2 Sew the outer border using EZBorder method.

3 Prepare the pillow backing and sew in place.

Fabric	Cut	For
Dark colored batik	1 square 9" x 9"	Background
Light colored batik	1 strip 1½" x 48"	Inner border
Batik print	1 strip 2½" x 60"	Outer border

Finishing the Pillow Back

1 Sew a ½" double hem along the long edge of each backing piece.

2 To assemble the backing, pin the cover backs to the pillow front, right sides together, matching the cut edges and overlapping the hemmed edges.

3 Sew all the seams.

4 Clip the corners and turn right-side out.

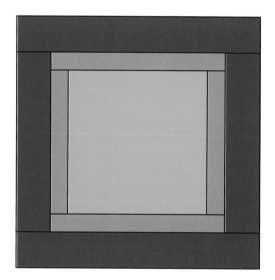

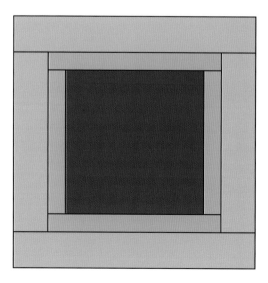

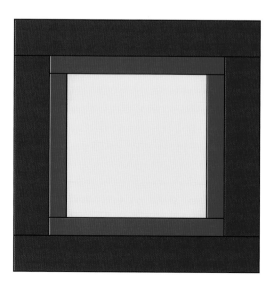

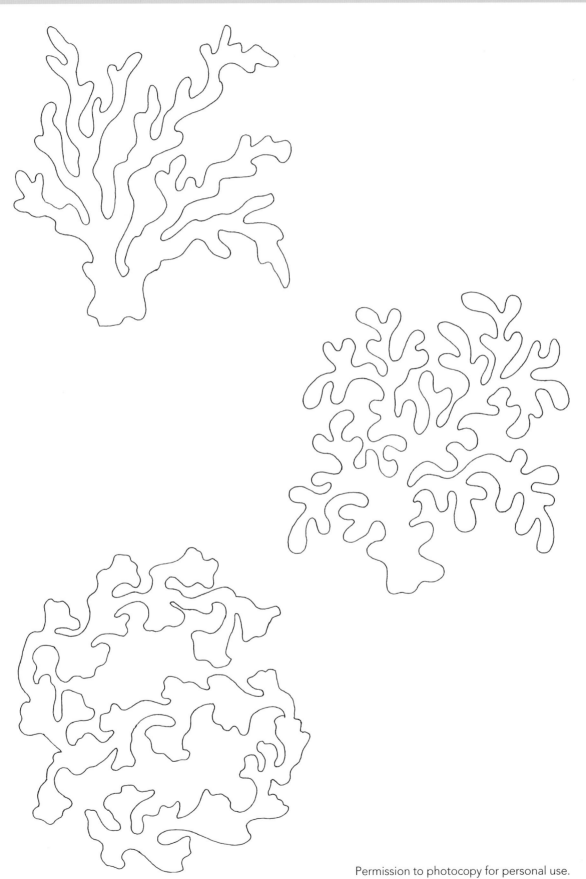

Asian Fronds

Shimmering silhouettes make an elegant statement when applied to a black background. The circular leaf motifs seem to float like delicate moons over a dark sea. When choosing fabric, select a multi-color print for the border, a one-color print for the leaves and a textured black for the background.

Finished size: 37" x 31"

Materials

Suggested colors:

1 yd. black for background

¾ yd. gold print for appliqué

¾ yd. multi-color print for borders

Backing 39" x 33"

Batting 39" x 33"

Monofilament thread for quilting

Refer to General Instructions on page 7 for assistance with basic sewing and quilting instruction.

Piecing

1 Sew the three black background panels together lengthwise with an EZBorder print strip between each piece and along both sides.

2 Sew an inner EZBorder print strip to the top and bottom of the quilt top.

3 Sew a black EZBorder around the quilt.

4 Sew a print EZBorder around the quilt.

Appliqué

1 Prepare the appliqué motifs using your favorite fusible method.

2 Assemble the motifs on the pieced background.

3 Press in place.

Fabric	Cut	For
Black	3 rectangles 10" x 24½"	Background
	1 strip 1" x 120"	Middle border
Multi-colored print	1 strip 1½" x 166"	Inner border
	1 strip 3½" x 136"	Outer border

Finishing

1 Layer the finished top, batting and backing.

2 Apply quilt basting spray.

3 This model was quilted in the ditch on the borders.

4 After quilting is complete, trim excess batting and backing.

5 Fold back the front outer border and hand sew the edges to the back side to finish.

Tip

This easy pattern lends itself to many looks by your selection of fabrics. My green sample block shows how three shades of leafy prints can create a lush tropical quilt. The same motif using watery, purple batiks looks like the leaves are floating on the sea at sunset. The trick is to select three contrasting prints or solids, keeping one color as the link to tie them together.

Color options for pillow using one of the Asian Fronds designs.

Love Anniversary Pillow

A handmade gift for a bridal shower, anniversary or someone special is most meaningfully treasured.
The pillow front is entirely fusible, and can be applied to a ready-made pillow for even faster results.
Fabric colors are soft for a pretty heirloom look.
Finished size: 13" x 11½" plus ruffle

Materials

Suggested colors:

Fat quarter textured white for the
background heart

Fat quarter soft green for the
background base, leaves and vines

Fat quarter soft lavender for the
flowers and "Love"

2 fat quarters of two shades of cream
for the bells and ribbon

1 yd. of white braided trim

Backing, two pieces 14" x 10"

12" pillow form or fiberfill

Fabric glue

The pillow itself uses the same soft green
fabric as the leaves. The ruffled border uses the
darker shade of cream fabric. You might choose
to purchase a pre-made lace ruffle for a more
feminine or country look.

Refer to General Instructions on page
7 for assistance with basic sewing and
quilting instruction.

Sewing the Pillow

(all sewing seams are ½" unless noted)

1 Matching right sides, sew the short edges of
the ruffle strip to form a large circle. To form
the ruffle, fold along the length with wrong
sides together and raw edges matching.
Press.

2 To gather the ruffle, machine baste ¼" from
the long raw edges of folded strip. Carefully
pull the thread ends drawing up gathers to
fit the pillow top.

3 Matching raw edges, baste the ruffle to
the right side of the pillow top, fitting the
corners into a curve.

4 To make the pillow back, fold back each
long edge of the pillow backing ½". Fold
½" again. Sew the folded seams flat.

5 Place the backing pieces right sides on the
pillow front and ruffle, matching raw edges
and overlapping the sewn edges to form
the envelope pillow back. Baste edges
through all layers.

6 Machine sew around the pillow. Turn the
pillow right-side out. Insert pillow form or
fiberfill.

Fabric	Cut	For
Soft green	1 rectangle 14" x 12½"	Front background base
Darker cream	1 strip 4" x 100"	Ruffle
Soft green	2 rectangles 9" x 12½"	Backing

Assembly

1 Cut out the white heart.

2 Prepare the appliqué shapes using your favorite fusible method.

3 Assemble the individual design pieces on the white heart.

4 Press in place.

5 Apply quilt basting spray to back side of the finished heart. Position the heart on the pillow front.

6 Apply a fine line of fabric glue to the back side of the braided trim as you place it around the raw edges of the heart. Let dry.

Tip

When working with words or numbers, before you prepare to fuse remember they must read right side up.

Baby Suit

Greet baby with a ducky banner in colors to brighten up the nursery. Our tiny green outfit will suit a boy's room. You might make the girl's outfit in pink and add some ruffles to the sleeves and leg openings. The baby's name could replace the word "baby."

Finished size: 12½" x 15½"

Materials

Suggested colors:

Fat quarter batiks or tiny prints in soft
   pink, blue, green, orange and yellow

Fat quarter white for background

Backing 14" x 17"

Batting 14" x 17"

Six white ½" buttons

½ yd. yellow ribbon

Monofilament thread for quilting

If baby's name has more letters, add more
squares to widen the wall hanging. To fill the
white background, make another suit or two, or
add a couple of yellow ducks swimming on blue
waves.

Refer to General Instructions on page
7 for assistance with basic sewing and
quilting instruction.

Piecing

1 Sew two sets of five squares in a row, mixing
the colors.

2 Sew two sets of six squares in a row, mixing
the colors.

3 Sew a five row unit to both sides of the
background block.

4 Sew a six row unit to the top and bottom
edges of the background block.

5 Sew the green border using EZBorder
method.

Appliqué

1 Prepare the appliqué shapes using your
favorite fusible method.

2 Assemble the individual design pieces on
the white background.

3 Press in place.

Fabric	Cut	For
Assorted batiks or tiny prints	22 squares 2½" x 2½"	Block border
White	1 rectangle 8" x 10½"	Background
Soft green	1 strip 2¼" x 62"	Outer border
Yellow	3 rectangles 1½" x 3"	Tabs

Finishing

1 Layer the finished top, batting and backing.

2 Apply quilt basting spray.

3 This model was quilted in the ditch on the borders.

4 After quilting is complete, trim excess batting and backing.

5 Fold back the border and hand sew the edges to the back side to finish.

6 Sew two white buttons to the bottom of the suit. Sew a button in the center of each corner square.

7 Make the hanging tabs. Using the three yellow rectangles, fold each tab in thirds lengthwise and top stitch on the fold. Fold the tabs in half, place on the back top edge of the banner and tack to secure.

Tip

Nobody cares if you can't quilt well. Just pull out your fabrics and quilt!

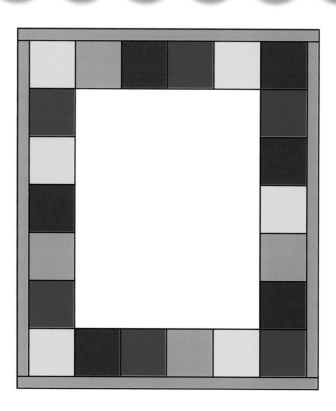

Petunia the Tooth Fairy and Oscar the Tooth Elf

When it's time for a tooth fairy visit, make it a special day with a charming banner.
Whether it's a cheery fairy for a little girl, or a mischievous elf for a boy, each holds a magical pouch
that's perfect to tuck in the loose tooth just before bedtime.
Finished size: 12" x 13" each

Materials

Suggested colors:

Fairy:

Fat quarter light yellow for background

Fat quarter gold for border

Elf:

Fat quarter light green for background

Fat quarter purple for border

For each fairy:

Fat quarter medium green for the
 inner borders

Scraps of assorted textured prints
 for the fairies

Blue glitter

Fabric glue

5 primary-colored star buttons,
 assorted sizes

2 primary-colored 1¼" buttons
 for hangers

Fine permanent black marker to draw
 the facial features

Batting 14" x 15"

Backing 14" x 15"

Monofilament thread for quilting

Scrap of iridescent sheer fabric for the
 tooth pouch

1 yd. metallic braid for pouch
 drawstring

Refer to General Instructions on page
7 for assistance with basic sewing and
quilting instruction.

For each banner

Fabric	Cut	For
Light green or yellow	1 square 9" x 9"	Background
Medium green	1 strip 1" x 44"	Inner border
Gold or purple	1 strip 2¼" x 56"	Outer border
Iridescent fabric	1 rectangle 5" x 10"	Tooth pouch

Piecing

1 Sew the inner border to the background using EZBorder method.

2 Sew the outer border using EZBorder method.

Appliqué

1 Prepare the appliqué shapes using your favorite fusible method.

2 Assemble the individual design pieces on the background.

3 Press in place.

4 Draw the smiles, eyes and nose with the black marker.

Finishing

1 Layer the finished front, batting and backing.

2 Apply quilt basting spray.

3 This model was quilted in the ditch along the borders.

4 When quilting is complete, trim excess batting and backing.

5 Fold back the outer border and hand sew the edges to the back side to finish.

6 Sew the star buttons to the banner, placing one button at the top of the fairy's hand.

7 Sew the large round buttons to the top left and right corners of the banner.

Tip

Embellishing is a terrific way to spice up a project. Any kind of trim, buttons or bows may be fused or glued with fabric glue to your project. Use the stitch options on your sewing machine to embroider or quilt the background. Sew some charms or glue some feathers. Use a rubber stamp dipped in acrylic paint to decorate the background fabric. Draw with colored pencils on the fabric. It's OK to try something different on a whimsical project if it makes you happy.

8 Squeeze a fine line of glue around the fairy wings. Sprinkle some glitter, or "magic dust" on the wet glue. Let dry before handling. Shake off excess glitter.

Pouch

1 Fold the iridescent rectangle in half widthwise. Sew the side seams.

2 Fold back the raw edge 1", wrong sides together. Machine sew ½" from the raw edge forming a casing.

3 Turn right-side out. Snip a small hole on the left and right fronts of the casing.

4 Cut the braid in half. Insert one braid end into the small hole and pull through the casing. Tie an overhand knot with the ends of braid forming a drawstring loop. Insert the second braid end into the opposite hole, and repeat.

5 The tooth pouch can be secured to the star on the fairy's hand.

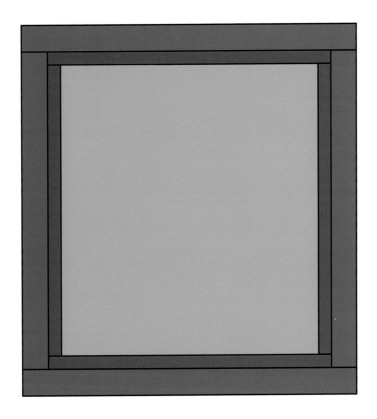

Permission to photocopy for personal use.

Hearts and Flowers Square

If you were to hand appliqué this traditional little square, it would take days to tuck and sew around each piece. Using fusibles, you can start this project in the morning and hang it on your wall by dinner time.

Finished size: 15" x 15"

Materials

Suggested colors:

Fat quarter medium green

Fat quarter medium pink

Fat quarter white for background

Batting 16" x 16"

Backing 16" x 16"

Monofilament thread for quilting

Refer to General Instructions on page 7 for assistance with basic sewing and quilting instruction.

Piecing

1 Sew two units each (B, E, C, E, B)

2 Sew two units each (E, C, E)

3 Sew the second two units to the sides of the A center square. Sew the first two units to the top and bottom sides of the center square.

4 Sew the inner pink border using EZBorder method.

5 Sew the white borders log cabin style.

6 Sew the outer pink borders using EZBorder method.

Appliqué

1 Prepare the appliqué shapes using your favorite fusible method.

2 Assemble the individual design pieces on the pieced background.

3 Press in place.

Fabric	Cut	For
White	1 square 4⅜" x 4⅜"	Unit A
	4 squares 2½" x 2½"	Unit B
	4 rectangles 2½" x 1¾"	Unit C
	4 strips 11½" x 2¾"	Unit D
Green	8 rectangles 2½" x 1¾"	Unit E
Pink	1 strip 1" x 40"	Inner border
	1 strip 1¾" x 64"	Outer border

Finishing

1 Layer the finished top, batting and backing.

2 Apply quilt basting spray.

3 This model was quilted in the ditch on the borders.

4 After quilting is complete, trim excess batting and backing.

5 Fold back the outer border and hand sew the edges to the back side to finish.

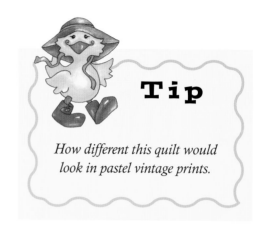

Tip

How different this quilt would look in pastel vintage prints.

Funky Nights

Here's a funky design made to brighten up your dining area.
If you'd like add place mats to coordinate on your table, use a few motifs scattered on the background.
Funky Nights would look great as a giant pillow for your teen's room. When your décor calls for softer
colors, choose earthy brown, moss green and gold to create a southwestern look.
Finished size: 22" x 22"

Materials

Fat quarters of strong colored batiks,
    red, sapphire, yellow, lime and purple
Black 24" x 24" for background
Backing 26" x 26"
Batting 26" x 26"
Monofilament thread for quilting
(Free Spirit fabrics were used)

Refer to General Instructions on page
7 for assistance with basic sewing and
quilting instruction.

Appliqué Cutting

1 Cut one large sun motif for the center of the square. Cut two each of the six motifs varying the colors. The border uses four squiggle motifs on each of the four sides, which are appliquéd. Choose any four fabric colors for the border, and cut four of each color.

Appliqué

1 Prepare the appliqué shapes using your favorite fusible method.

2 Assemble the individual motifs on the black background as shown.

3 Press in place.

Fabric	Cut	For
Black	1 square 24" x 24"	Background

Finishing

1 Layer the finished front, batting and backing.

2 Apply quilt basting spray.

3 Quilt as desired. This model echoed the square spiral motif in a free form quilting pattern. Leave 2" along each edge unquilted to allow for turning.

4 After your quilting is complete, evenly trim the excess edges of the batting and backing.

5 Fold back the quilt front and hand sew the edges to the back side to finish.

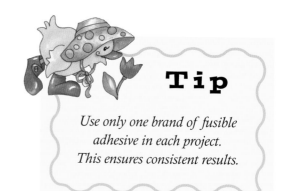

Tip

Use only one brand of fusible adhesive in each project. This ensures consistent results.

Hot Flash Pillow

Some very wild batik prints, and a very cool fabric ribbon inspired this hot pillow.
The ¾"-wide fabric strips come in skeins ready to use for crafts, knit or crochet. I chose this
black and white print ribbon to make a fabulous fringe on a pillow with abstract designs.
Finished size of pillow: 12" x 12", plus fringe

Materials

Suggested colors:

Fat quarter black for appliqué

Fat quarter black/orange abstract print
   for border and appliqué

Fat quarter orange batik for
   background

2 skeins of ¾" wide fabric ribbon

Hole punch tool

Large crochet hook

Fiberfill

(Princess Mirah Bali fabrics were used)

Refer to General Instructions on page 7 for assistance with basic sewing and quilting instruction.

Appliqué

1 Prepare the appliqué shapes using your favorite fusible method.

2 Assemble the individual design pieces on each background squares.

3 Press in place.

Tip

Inspiration appears in the most unexpected places. Write it down, take a photo or share it with a friend, so you don't forget it.

Fabric	Cut	For
Orange batik	2 squares 12" x 12"	Background
Black/orange abstract print	1 strip 3" x 52"	Border

Assembly

1 With right sides together, sew the pillow seams leaving a 6" opening.

2 Turn right-side out.

3 Fold the border in half lengthwise and baste to the front of the pillow, raw edges facing towards the center of the pillow and allowing ¾" of the folded border edge to extend beyond the pillow. Topstitch to the pillow.

4 With the hole punch tool, punch a row of holes through the folded fabric border about 1¼" apart.

5 To make the fringe, cut 12" lengths of fabric ribbon with a diagonal cut on the ends. Fold two strips in half, pull strips halfway through the hole from the back side with the crochet hook. Insert the ends into the loop. Pull ends slightly to tighten into a knot. Repeat in all the holes.

6 Stuff the pillow with fiberfill. Hand sew the opening closed.

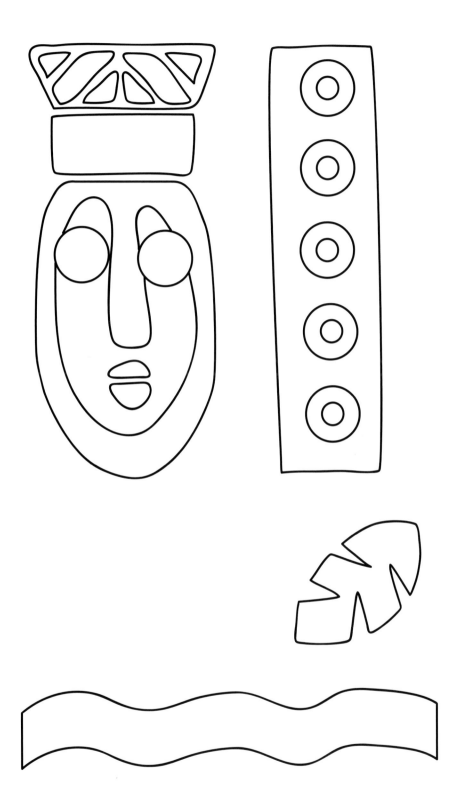

Mitten Row

At the end of every winter season, we seem to acquire a collection of single mittens...
little orphans just waiting for a hand to dance. Place this cheerful banner at your back door
to remind your family to keep track of their own mittens.

Finished size: 29" x 15"

Materials

Suggested colors:

Fat quarters of bright blue, red, black,
   green, purple in funky textured
   prints for the mittens

½ yd. black for borders

⅓ yd. medium gold background

Backing 30" x 16"

Batting 30" x 16"

Assortment of red buttons

Iron-on red metallic #16 braid (Kreinik)

Glue Dots

Monofilament thread for quilting

Refer to General Instructions on page
7 for assistance with basic sewing and
quilting instruction.

Piecing

1 Sew the entire length of the black inner
border to the red border.

2 Sew the border unit to the top edge of the
gold background, placing the black against
the gold fabric.

3 Trim the ends even with the sides of the
gold background.

4 Sew a blue square to the end of the
remaining border unit.

5 Align the blue corner and border
unit against the right side of the gold
background and sew. Repeat for the bottom
and left side. A small seam and a blue
corner square are needed to connect the
left side border to the top border.

6 Sew the black outer border using EZBorder
method.

Fabric	Cut	For
Blue	4 squares 2¾" x 2¾"	Corner squares
Black	1 strip 1¼" x 120"	Inner border
	1 strip 2" x 180"	Outer border
Red	1 strip 2" x 120"	Middle border
Medium gold	1 rectangle 24" x 10"	Background

Appliqué

1 Prepare the appliqué shapes using your favorite fusible method.

2 Assemble the individual design pieces on the gold background.

3 Press in place.

4 Following manufacturer's instructions, lay the red braid playfully across the tops of the mittens and iron in place. (You may use any kind of ribbon or trim instead, and use fabric glue to secure it to the background.)

Finishing

1 Layer the finished top, batting and backing.

2 Apply the quilt basting spray.

3 This model was quilted in a free form swirly pattern.

4 After quilting is complete, fold back the black border and hand sew to the back side finish.

5 Apply a glue dot to the back of each button and randomly arrange along the braid, pressing in place with your finger.

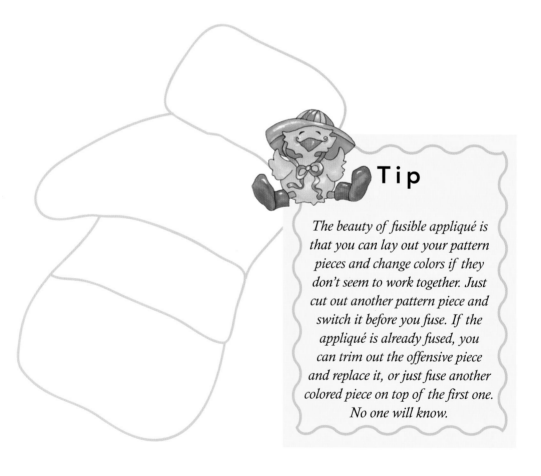

Tip

The beauty of fusible appliqué is that you can lay out your pattern pieces and change colors if they don't seem to work together. Just cut out another pattern piece and switch it before you fuse. If the appliqué is already fused, you can trim out the offensive piece and replace it, or just fuse another colored piece on top of the first one. No one will know.

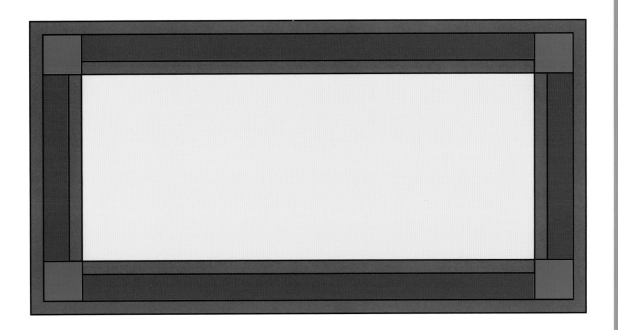

Melt Your Heart Snowmen Pillow

With lots of warm colors and cheerful smiles, this snowman trio pillow will certainly bring you smiles on a brisk cold day. Fat quarters and scraps are all you need to sew this pillow in a jiffy. The fabric colors you select should be strong and dark against a crisp white background. The fabric prints for the hats and scarves could have some textures that one might find on knitted items.

Finished size: 14" x 14"

Materials

Suggested colors:

Fat quarters of lime green, dark blue, dark red, medium red, medium yellow for the hats and scarves

Scrap of light pink for the cheeks

Scrap of orange for the noses

Scrap of black for the eyes

Fat quarter white (background)

Dark red (backing)
  2 pieces 14½" x 10" each

14" x 14" pillow form or fiberfill

Black fine permanent marker to draw the smiles

4 white buttons, 1" each

Refer to General Instructions on page 7 for assistance with basic sewing and quilting instruction.

Appliqué

1 Prepare the appliqué shapes using your favorite fusible method.

2 Assemble the individual design pieces on the white background square.

3 Press in place.

4 Draw the smiles with the marker as shown.

Piecing

1 Sew the blue and red borders with EZBorders.

2 Press the borders.

3 Prepare the pillow backing and sew in place.

Fabric	Cut	For
White	1 square 10" x 10"	Background
Dark blue	1 strip 2" x 48"	Inner border
Medium red	1 strip 1½" x 60"	Outer border

Finishing the Pillow Back

1 Sew a ½" double hem along one long edge of each backing piece.

2 To assemble the backing, pin the cover backs to the pillow front, right sides together, matching the cut edges and overlapping the hemmed edges.

3 Sew all the seams.

4 Clip the corners and turn right-sides out.

5 Insert pillow form.

6 Sew a white button at each corner.

Tip

Shopping for fabric is more fun with a friend.

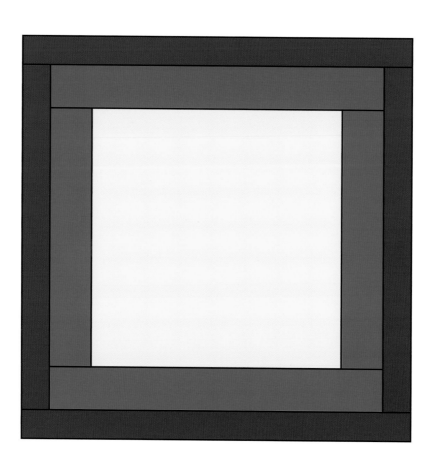

Jolly Snowmen Row

Mr. Frosty and friends, dressed in their woolies and lined up in a row, love the cold winter days.
Choose bright colors in tiny prints for the hats and jackets.
A frosted white fabric will make the snowmen's bodies shimmer.
Finished size: 36" x 14½"

Materials

Fat quarters or scraps of bright red,
yellow, green, blue and black
in finely textured prints for the
outerwear

Scraps of light pink for the cheeks

Scraps of orange for the noses

Scraps of white for the bodies

½ yd. light blue for background

Fat quarter white (inner border)

Fat quarter medium blue (border)

Fine black permanent marker to
draw the smiles and eyes

Batting 38" x 16"

Backing 38" x 16"

Light blue 100% cotton thread for
quilting

Refer to General Instructions on page
7 for assistance with basic sewing and
quilting instruction.

Piecing

1 Sew the white inner border to the light blue
background using EZBorder method.

2 Sew the medium blue outer border using
EZBorder method.

Appliqué

1 Prepare the appliqué shapes using your
favorite fusible method.

2 Assemble the individual design pieces on
the light blue background.

3 Press in place.

4 Draw the smiles with the marker as shown.

Fabric	Cut	For
Light blue	1 rectangle 33" x 10½"	Background
White	1 strip 2¼" x 84"	Inner border
Medium blue	1 strip 2¼" x 160"	Outer border

Finishing

1 Layer the finished top, batting and backing.

2 Apply quilt basting spray.

3 This model has the snowmen outline quilted and flowing quilting lines on the borders.

4 When quilting is complete, trim the excess batting and backing.

5 Fold back the outer border, and hand sew the edges to the back side to finish.

Tip

When you have chosen the colors for appliqué pieces and placed them on your background, you may find that a shape seems to blend into the background, as in the white snowmen bodies on a light blue background. It's okay to take a good quality color pencil to shade the edges of your appliqué piece. I've used a medium value blue/gray color pencil to outline the white snowmen shapes and added a little shading to round out the bodies.

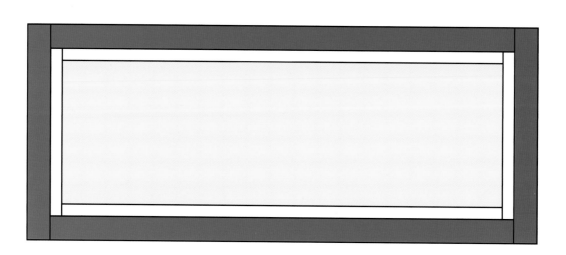

Snowflakes

Inspired by the paper snowflake cutouts made by children, it is just as easy to make cutout fabric snowflakes. When the design is traced on the paper backing of the fusible adhesive, it takes no time at all to cut out the snowflakes.

Finished size: 43 " x 12¾"

Materials

Suggested colors:

1 fat quarter each of frosty white and crisp dark blue (background)

Fat quarter of a colorful print (border)

Batting 45" x 15"

Backing 45" x 15"

Monofilament thread for quilting

Refer to General Instructions on page 7 for assistance with basic sewing and quilting instruction.

Piecing

1 Sew a white square to each side of the blue square.

2 Sew a border strip to the top and bottom edges of the row of squares.

3 Sew a border strip to a short side of the triangle, aligning the 90-degree angle end flush, and allowing 2¼" of the border to extend beyond the opposite pointed end.

4 Sew another border strip to the triangle unit, aligning ends in the same manner. Repeat on the second triangle.

5 Place the end units at the ends of the row. Sew in place.

Assembly

1 Prepare the appliqué shapes using your favorite fusible method.

2 Assemble the snowflakes on the background.

3 Press in place.

Fabric	Cut	For
White	2 squares 10¼" x 10¼"	Background
Blue	1 square 10¼" x 10¼"	Background
	1 square 7¼" x 7¼"	End triangles
	Cut square diagonally to make 2 triangles	
Multi-print	1 strip 2¼" x 90"	Border

Finishing

1 Layer the finished top, batting and backing.

2 Trim the excess batting and backing.

3 Fold back the border, and hand sew the edges to the back side to finish.

Tip

The snowflakes would make wonderful pillow ornaments in a small size and with frosted fabrics.

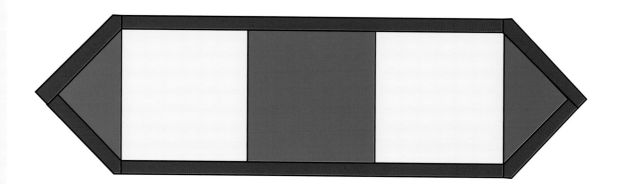

Whimsical Hats

Make any day brighter with a cheery hat and a little friend. Winter, spring, summer and fall ... a hat for all seasons! The bright colors stand strong against the funky printed background squares and borders. Enlarge a design to make a flag or banner, or select one motif and repeat it in different colors for a fun mini-quilt.
Finished size: 27" x 27"

Materials

Suggested colors:

Fat quarters of bold, batiks in yellow, orange, blue, aqua, red, lime, green, purple and black

¾ yd. white print (background)

½ yd. black print (outer border)

4 fat quarters for inner borders in colors to match the motifs

Fat quarter for binding in your favorite color

Batting 29" x 29"

Backing 29" x 29"

Monofilament thread for quilting

Refer to General Instructions on page 7 for assistance with basic sewing and quilting instruction.

Piecing

1 Sew inner borders to each background square using EZBorder method.

2 Sew a row (square, black outer border, square) and repeat with the second set of squares.

3 Sew a black border between the two sets of rows to form the quilt.

4 Sew the black outer borders using EZBorder method.

5 Sew the binding using EZBorder method.

Fabric	Cut	For
White print	4 squares 10½" x 10½"	Background
Blue	1 strip 1¼" x 48"	Inner border
Lime	1 strip 1¼" x 48"	Inner border
Purple	1 strip 1¼" x 48"	Inner border
Red	1 strip 1¼" x 48"	Inner border
Black	1 strip 1¾" x 170"	Outer border
White	1 strip 1½" x 120"	Binding

Assembly

1 Prepare the appliqué shapes using your favorite fusible method. See Tip.

2 Assemble the individual design pieces on the squares.

3 Press in place.

Finishing

1 Layer the finished top, batting and backing.

2 Apply quilt basting spray.

3 This model was quilted in the ditch on the borders and around the hat motifs.

4 After quilting is complete, trim excess batting and backing.

5 Fold back the binding and hand sew the edges to the back side to finish.

Tip

If your appliqué motifs seem to get "lost" on a printed background, fuse the appliqué shapes on a solid color fabric that coordinate with the design. Trim the solid fabric as a halo around the motif and then apply it to the printed background. This technique will contain the design as a stronger unit and add even more color to your quilt.

My Dancing Hearts

I have been blessed to have the love-of-my-life with me for over 25 years. For a special anniversary gift,
I made this delightful little banner to place in our breakfast nook and to remind me of how much
my husband must love me to bear with me for so long.

Finished size: 13½" x 20½"

Materials

Suggested colors:

Fat quarters of several prints of red, blue and yellow for the assorted hearts and border

⅓ yd. of very light lavender batik for background

¼ yd. medium blue for the binding

Batting 15" x 22"

Backing 15" x 22"

Assorted ribbon scraps

Assorted colored buttons

Monofilament thread for quilting

Refer to General Instructions on page 7 for assistance with basic sewing and quilting instruction.

Piecing

1 Sew the assortment of rectangles in a row, matching the long side right sides together to make a 20" length of joined rectangles.

2 Place the rectangle row section, right sides together, on a long side of the backing. Sew the seam.

3 Sew the blue binding using EZBorder method.

Assembly

1 Prepare the applique shapes using your favorite fusible method. This pattern uses an assortment of heart appliques.

2 Assemble the individual design pieces on the background.

3 Press in place.

Fabric	Cut	For
Very light lavender	1 rectangle 10" x 20"	Background
Medium blue	1 strip 1¾" x 70"	Binding
Assorted prints of red, blue and yellow	assorted rectangles 1" x 3½" to 2½" x 3½"	Rectangle strip

Finishing

1 Layer the finished top, batting and backing.

2 Apply quilt basting spray.

3 This model was quilted in free form hearts and squiggly vertical lines to suggest hangers for the hearts.

4 After quilting is complete, trim excess batting and backing.

5 Fold back the front outer border and hand sew the edges to the back side to finish.

Dangling Hearts

1 Prepare three dangling hearts using instructions for Two Sided Applique on page 12.

2 Cut three ribbon pieces in different lengths for hangers.

3 Glue a ribbon to the back of each heart and to the bottom edge of the quilt. See photo on page 116.

Embellish

1 Add buttons and ribbon bows to several of the hearts as desired. Secure with fabric glue.

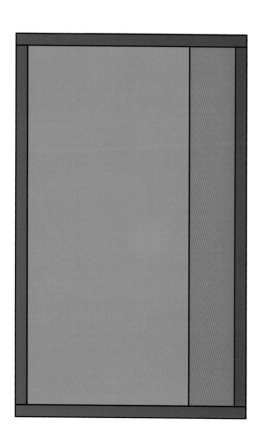

Tip

When making a gift for a friend, don't forget the love.

Sunny Poppy Club

Nothing cheers me up like a cluster of red flowers. Like bobbing balloons on slender green stems, poppies bring to mind happy childhood days walking hand-in-hand with grandma to her bountiful garden.

Finished size: 25½" x 21½"

Materials

Suggested colors:

Fat quarters of assorted prints of
medium red for the poppies

Fat quarters of medium green for the
leaves and stems

½ yd. light yellow print or batik
for the background

¼ yd. medium green print for
the binding

Batting 27" x 23"

Backing 27" x 23"

Monofilament thread for quilting

Refer to General Instructions on page
7 for assistance with basic sewing and
quilting instruction.

Piecing

1 Sew the red border using EZBorder method
around the light yellow center section.

2 Sew the green binding using EZBorder
method.

Assembly

1 Prepare the appliqué shapes using your
favorite fusible method.

2 Arrange the individual poppy, stem and leaf
pieces on the center section.

3 Press in place.

Fabric	Cut	For
Light yellow	1 rectangle 21" x 17"	Background
Medium red	1 strip 1¼" x 84"	Border
Medium green	1 strip 3¼" x 96"	Binding

Finishing

1 Layer the finished top, batting and backing.

2 Apply quilt basting spray.

3 This model was quilted in a free form style to complement the poppies.

4 After quilting is complete, trim excess batting and backing.

5 Fold back the front outer border and hand sew the edges to the back side to finish.

Tip

Do you like a pattern, but the colors aren't right for you? Think how lovely this design would look with a dark blue background and white appliquéd poppies, or sunny yellow poppies dancing on sky blue fabric.

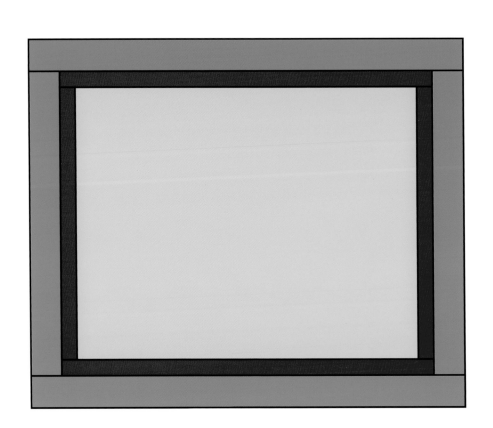

How to Use the CD-ROM

The enclosed CD has all the appliqué designs used in this book. Just print out the number of copies you will need for each project and start appliquéing.

If you do not have access to a computer, check with your local copy or print shop and ask if they could print out the designs for you to have as originals. They may charge a minimal fee for this but it will be worth it. Or, if you have a friend, son, daughter or grandchild, ask them to print copies out for you.

Steps

1 Insert CD into CD drive.

2 Open CD.

3 Open file name.

4 Print out the number of copies you would like for each project.

If you have an inkjet printer and fusible product that is 8½" x 11", you can print the designs onto the fusible paper. This only works with an inkjet printer <u>NOT</u> a laser printer, because an inkjet printer doesn't use heat to bond the ink as a laser printer does.

About the Author

Ursula Michael's delightful designs for needlework have charmed stitchers for over 25 years. Combining her love of working with needle and thread, and art to make you smile, Ursula started designing in the 70s with traditional quilts for publications, moved on to crochet, discovered cross stitch and needlework, indulged in graphic art, and has come full circle to quilts again. This time around, her light-hearted applique quilts use today's newest products to make quilting friendly for everyone.

Living on a small coastal island in little Rhode Island, Ursula shares her home with her husband Al and Maverick, her big black dog. Together they spend as much time as they can by the ocean collecting treasures, boating and sprawled in their beach chairs to daydream.

Resources

Fabric

FreeSpirit
www.freespiritfabric.com
1-888-217-1215

Starr Design Fabrics
www.starrfabrics.com
530-467-5121

Bali Fabrics
www.balifab.com
1-800-783-4612

Quilt Basting Spray

Sullivans USA
www.sullivans.net
1-800-862-8586

Thread

WonderFil Specialty Threads
www.wonderfil.net
403 250-8262 (Canada)

Sulky
www.sulky.com
770 429-3979

YLI
www.ylicorp.com
803 985-3100

Kreinik
www.kreinik.com
800 624-1928

Batting

Airtex
www.airtex.com
1-800-851-8887

Fusible Adhesive

HeatnBond Ultrahold Iron On Adhesive
www.thermoweb.com
1-800-323-0799

Esterita Austin's Misty Fuse
www.EsteritaAustin.com

Steam-A-Seam
The Warm Company
www.warmcompany.com
1-800-234-WARM

Computer Printer Fabric

June Tailor
www.junetailor.com

Colored Pencils

Prismacolor Pencils
www.prismacolor.com

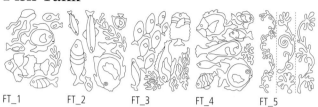

CD-ROM Index

Fish Tank

FT_1   FT_2   FT_3   FT_4   FT_5

Rainy Day Umbrella

RDU_1

Heart Maze

HM_1

Sea Life

SL_1   SL_2   SL_3   SL_4   SL_5   SL_6   SL_7   SL_8

My Dancing Hearts

MDH_1

Scallop Festival Quilt

SFQ_1   SFQ_2

Umbrella Dance

UD_1   UD_2   UD_3

Baby Suit

BS_1

Butterfly Windows

BW_1   BW_2   BW_3   BW_4

Four Seasons

FS_1   FS_2   FS_3   FS_4

Welcome Kittens

WK_W   WK_E1   WK_L   WK_C   WK_O   WK_M   WK_E2

Happy Hour

HH_1   HH_2

Redwork Place Mats

RW_1   RW_2   RW_3

Coral Pillows

CP_1   CP_2   CP_3

Asian Fronds

AF_1   AF_2   AF_3   AF_4   AF_5   AF_6   AF_7   AF_8   AF_9

Love Anniversary Pillow

Snowflakes

LAP_1   LAP_2   LAP_3   SNF_1   SNF_2   SNF_3

Petunia the Tooth Fairy and Oscar the Tooth Elf

Melt Your Heart Snowman Pillow

Hearts and Flowers Square

TF_1   TF_2   SMP_1   HFS_1

Hot Flash Pillow

Mitten Row

Funky Nights

HF_1   HF_2   MR_1   FN_1   FN_2   FN_3

Jolly Snowman Row

Sunny Poppy Club

JSR_1   JSR_2   JSR_3   JSR_4   JSR_5

SPC_1A
SPC_1B
SPC_1C
SPC_2A
SPC_2B
SPC_2C

Whimsical Hats

Alphabet

WH_1   WH_2   WH_3   WH_4   ALPHA_1   ALPHA_2   ALPHA_3   ALPHA_4

Expand Your Quick Project Possibilities

Low-Sew Boutique
*25 Quick & Clever Projects
Using Ready-Mades*
by Cheryl Weiderspahn

Transform common placements, towels, potholders and rugs into 25+ innovative fashion accessories, such as a backpack, eyeglass case, purse and more, by following the detailed instructions and 175 color photos and illustrations in this unique guide.

Softcover • 8¼ x 10⅞ • 128 pages
175 color photos
Item# Z0378 • $22.99

Raggedy Reverse Appliqué
*10 Fast, Fun and Forgiving
Quilt Projects*
by Kim Deneault

Discover a stress-free new appliqué technique in the detailed instructions and 175 color photos and illustrations of this book. Plus, you'll find 10 projects for small and quick projects, as well as more complex projects, featured on a pattern insert.

Softcover • 8¼ x 10⅞ • 128 pages
25 b&w illus. • 175 color photos
Item# Z0765 • $24.99

One Stitch™ Quilting: The Basics
20 Fun Projects You Can Finish in a Day
by Donna Dewberry and Cindy Casciato

Create stylish quilt projects in less time with the innovative new quilting method represented in more than 300 color photos and illustrations, and demonstrated in 20 exciting projects included in this book.

Softcover • 8¼ x 10⅞ • 128 pages
300 color photos
Item# OSQB • $22.99

90-Minute Quilts
*25+ Projects You Can Make
in an Afternoon*
by Meryl Ann Butler

Discover how easy it is to create stylish baby and large lap quilts, plus wall hangings using the quick tips, methods and 250 how-to color photos and illustrations included in this book.

Hardcover • 8 x 8 • 160 pages
250 color photos and illus.
Item# NTYMQ • $24.99

Crazy Shortcut Quilts
*Quilt as You Go and Finish
in Half the Time!*
by Marguerita McManus and Sarah Raffuse

Extend your quilting skills and passion into the limitless world of home décor, with the step-by-step instructions and 175 color photos featured in this book.

Softcover • 8¼ x 10⅞ • 128 pages
50 b&w illus. • 175 color photos
Item# Z0973 • $22.99